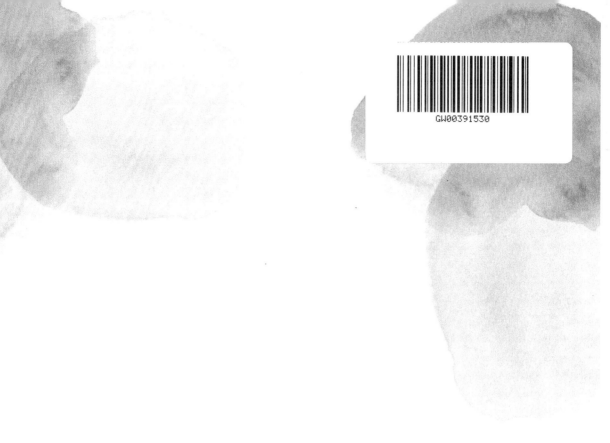

The Optimism
JOURNAL

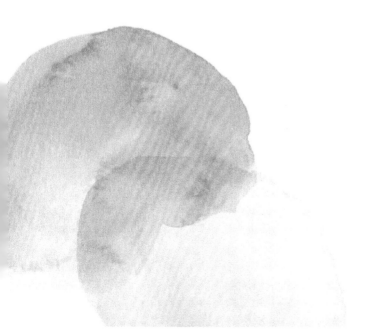

A Daily Prayer

Never give up; don't give in
Though skies seem cloudy and grey,
Keep on smiling, keep the faith,
Each tomorrow's a new day

Just as plants need rain and sun
To thrive and look their best
So we all have to face dark clouds
If we are to pass Life's test

So head down, chin up and battle through,
Stay resolute and true,
Your Guardian Angel's by your side
To bring you smiling through

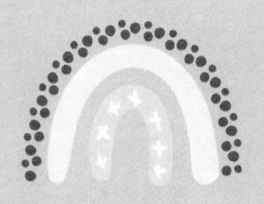

BE PATiENT WiTH ME...

I'm a work in progress

Date today:

Something I achieved:

Something that made me smile:

Something I learned:

Something I'm looking forward to:

Something I enjoyed:

Three things I'm grateful for:

My Thoughts:

If you wouldn't say it to a friend, why say it to Yourself?

Date today:

Something I achieved:

Something that made me smile:

Something I learned:

Something I'm looking forward to:

Something I enjoyed:

Three things I'm grateful for:

....

....

....

My Thoughts:

....

....

....

....

You don't have to do it on your own - just reach out

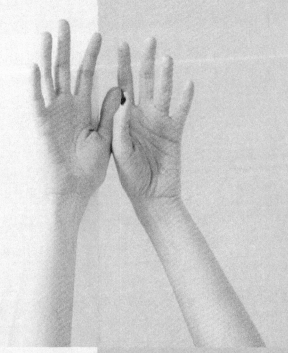

Date today:

Something I achieved:

Something that made me smile:

Something I learned:

Something I'm looking forward to:

Something I enjoyed:

Three things I'm grateful for:
....
....
....

My Thoughts:
....
....
....
....

If at first you don't
succeed , try another way

Date today:

Something I achieved:

Something that made me smile:

Something I learned:

Something I'm looking forward to:

Something I enjoyed:

Three things I'm grateful for:
....
....
....

My Thoughts:
....
....
....
....

Nothing is a failure

It's just

another way

of doing it

Date today:

Something I achieved:

Something that made me smile:

Something I learned:

Something I'm looking forward to:

Something I enjoyed:

Three things I'm grateful for:

My Thoughts:

A dream

fulfilled

....is like a tree in

blossom

Date today:

Something I achieved:

Something that made me smile:

Something I learned:

Something I'm looking forward to:

Something I enjoyed:

Three things I'm grateful for:

....

....

....

My Thoughts:

....

....

....

....

BE HAPPY: IT'S CATCHING

Date today:

Something I achieved:

Something that made me smile:

Something I learned:

Something I'm looking forward to:

Something I enjoyed:

Three things I'm grateful for:

....

....

....

My Thoughts:

....

....

....

....

EVERYTHING
WILL TURN
OUT WELL IN
THE END...

...IF IT'S NOT
WELL, IT'S
NOT THE END

John Lennon

Date today:

Something I achieved:

Something that made me smile:

Something I learned:

Something I'm looking forward to:

Something I enjoyed:

Three things I'm grateful for:
....
....
....

My Thoughts:
....
....
....
....

A happy heart...

Makes the face beautiful

Date today:

Something I achieved:

Something that made me smile:

Something I learned:

Something I'm looking forward to:

Something I enjoyed:

Three things I'm grateful for:

My Thoughts:

Arguing with a fool
just makes
two fools.

Date today:

Something I achieved:

Something that made me smile:

Something I learned:

Something I'm looking forward to:

Something I enjoyed:

Three things I'm grateful for:

....

....

....

My Thoughts:

....

....

....

....

Everyone has a talent

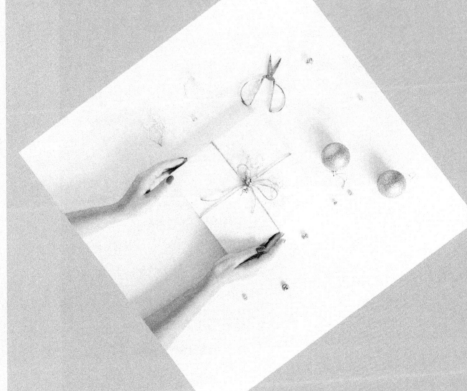

... the real skill lies in
discovering what it is

Date today:

Something I achieved:

Something that made me smile:

Something I learned:

Something I'm looking forward to:

Something I enjoyed:

Three things I'm grateful for:

My Thoughts:

One day into a dark time

Is one day nearer
the end

Date today:

Something I achieved:

Something that made me smile:

Something I learned:

Something I'm looking forward to:

Something I enjoyed:

Three things I'm grateful for:

My Thoughts:

Don't take on the world

Just your little bit of it

Date today:

Something I achieved:

Something that made me smile:

Something I learned:

Something I'm looking forward to:

Something I enjoyed:

Three things I'm grateful for:

My Thoughts:

Sometimes it's only after the storm that we appreciate the sun

Date today:

Something I achieved:

Something that made me smile:

Something I learned:

Something I'm looking forward to:

Something I enjoyed:

Three things I'm grateful for:
....
....
....

My Thoughts:
....
....
....
....

Remember rainbows are made with sunshine AND rain

Date today:

Something I achieved:

Something that made me smile:

Something I learned:

Something I'm looking forward to:

Something I enjoyed:

Three things I'm grateful for:
....
....
....

My Thoughts:
....
....
....
....

STOP FOR A WHILE AND LISTEN
TO THE BEAT OF A
BUTTERFLY'S WING

Date today:

Something I achieved:

Something that made me smile:

Something I learned:

Something I'm looking forward to:

Something I enjoyed:

Three things I'm grateful for:
....
....
....

My Thoughts:
....
....
....
....

take heart...
perhaps it's just not
the right time

Date today:

Something I achieved:

Something that made me smile:

Something I learned:

Something I'm looking forward to:

Something I enjoyed:

Three things I'm grateful for:
....
....
....

My Thoughts:
....
....
....
....

Life is for being not doing

Date today:

Something I achieved:

Something that made me smile:

Something I learned:

Something I'm looking forward to:

Something I enjoyed:

Three things I'm grateful for:

....

....

....

My Thoughts:

....

....

....

....

Today is a new
chapter in my
story : what shall
I write?

Date today:

Something I achieved:

Something that made me smile:

Something I learned:

Something I'm looking forward to:

Something I enjoyed:

Three things I'm grateful for:

....
....
....

My Thoughts:

....
....
....
....

Do one thing every day
that scares you

Eleanor Roosevelt

Date today:

Something I achieved:

Something that made me smile:

Something I learned:

Something I'm looking forward to:

Something I enjoyed:

Three things I'm grateful for:

....

....

....

My Thoughts:

....

....

....

....

You can climb the highest hill

...just one step at a time

Date today:

Something I achieved:

Something that made me smile:

Something I learned:

Something I'm looking forward to:

Something I enjoyed:

Three things I'm grateful for:

My Thoughts:

You

can

only

do the

best

you

can

with the knowledge you

have at the time

Date today:

Something I achieved:

Something that made me smile:

Something I learned:

Something I'm looking forward to:

Something I enjoyed:

Three things I'm grateful for:

....

....

....

My Thoughts:

....

....

....

....

It's sometimes easier to ask for forgiveness than permission

Date today:

Something I achieved:

Something that made me smile:

Something I learned:

Something I'm looking forward to:

Something I enjoyed:

Three things I'm grateful for:

....

....

....

My Thoughts:

....

....

....

....

HAPPINESS

*isn't journey's end
but the journey*

Date today:

Something I achieved:

Something that made me smile:

Something I learned:

Something I'm looking forward to:

Something I enjoyed:

Three things I'm grateful for:
....
....
....

My Thoughts:
....
....
....
....

Many years of life...

...are made up of many little

moments

Date today:

Something I achieved:

Something that made me smile:

Something I learned:

Something I'm looking forward to:

Something I enjoyed:

Three things I'm grateful for:

My Thoughts:

How can You find the desert island if yOu never leave the shOre?

Date today:

Something I achieved:

Something that made me smile:

Something I learned:

Something I'm looking forward to:

Something I enjoyed:

Three things I'm grateful for:

....

....

....

My Thoughts:

....

....

....

....

What a caterpillar calls the end, the
rest of the world calls a butterfly

Lao Tzu

Date today:

Something I achieved:

Something that made me smile:

Something I learned:

Something I'm looking forward to:

Something I enjoyed:

Three things I'm grateful for:

....
....
....

My Thoughts:

....
....
....
....

STOP,
TAKE A BREATH

AND SEE THE UNIVERSE
SMILE AROUND YOU

Date today:

Something I achieved:

Something that made me smile:

Something I learned:

Something I'm looking forward to:

Something I enjoyed:

Three things I'm grateful for:

My Thoughts:

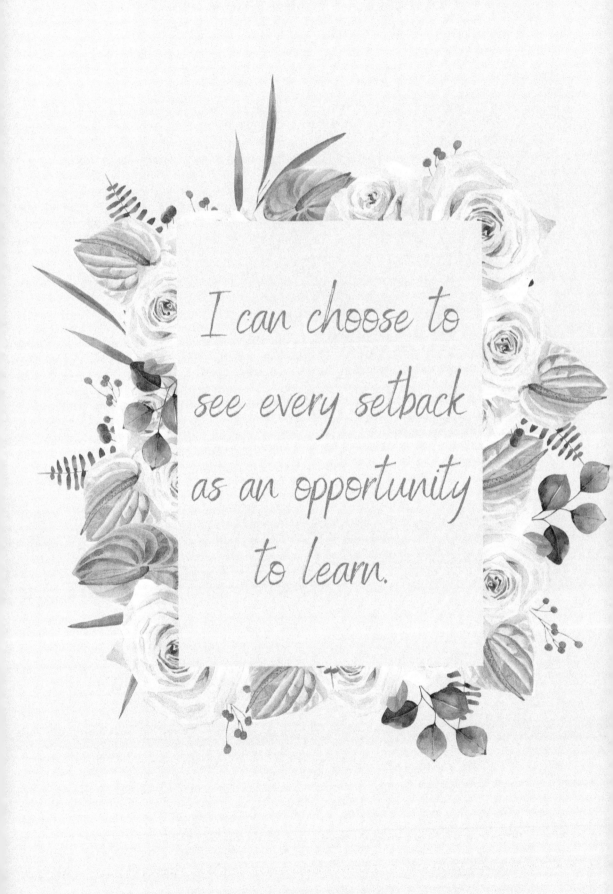

I can choose to see every setback as an opportunity to learn.

Date today:

Something I achieved:

Something that made me smile:

Something I learned:

Something I'm looking forward to:

Something I enjoyed:

Three things I'm grateful for:

....
....
....

My Thoughts:

....
....
....
....

We're weaving rich tapestries of
life but we can only see them
from the back with all the knots
and loose ends

Date today:

Something I achieved:

Something that made me smile:

Something I learned:

Something I'm looking forward to:

Something I enjoyed:

Three things I'm grateful for:

....

....

....

My Thoughts:

....

....

....

....

My thoughts

My thoughts

My thoughts

My thoughts

My thoughts

My thoughts

My thoughts

My thoughts

My thoughts

My thoughts

My thoughts

My thoughts

My thoughts

My thoughts

My Thoughts

My thoughts

My thoughts

My thoughts

My thoughts

My thoughts

My thoughts

Printed in Great Britain
by Amazon